THE
BIG
BOOK
OF
CHIC

MILES REDD

THE BIG BOOK OF CHIC

ASSOULINE

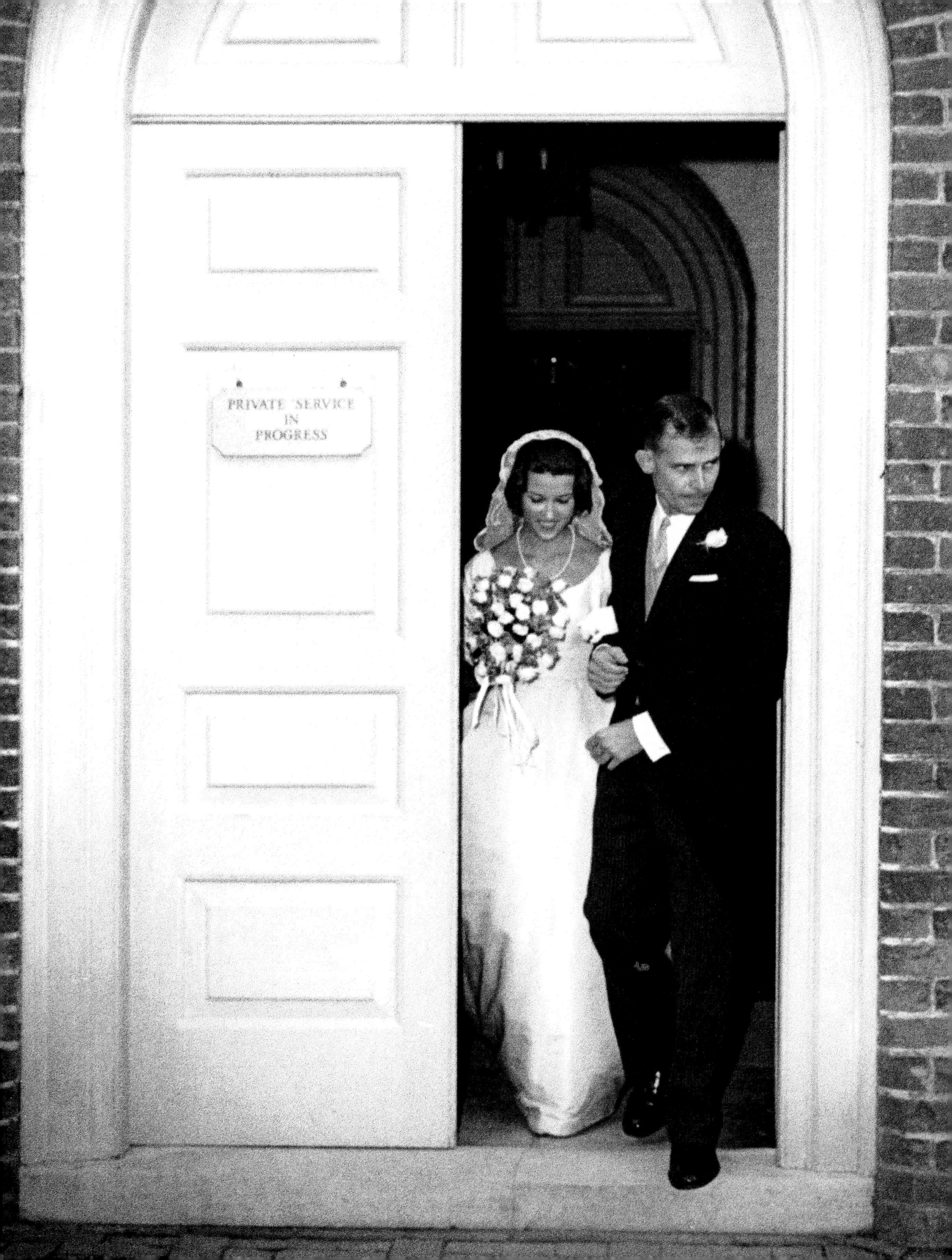
PRIVATE SERVICE
IN
PROGRESS

For my mother and father,

who gave me this wonderful life.

When I was a boy growing up in Atlanta, Georgia, my mother had a copy of Cecil Beaton's book *The Royal Portraits* that I used to flip through for hours on end. The photographs are heady stuff: Princess Elizabeth in ermine coronation robes, holding scepters; Princess Margaret in an immense tulle ball gown splayed across a red damask banquette. After that, there wasn't a prayer for me; my five-year-old eyes had seen what appeared to be the height of chic, and there was no turning back, at least not until I had my own tufted red madness. It was my first glimpse of the great big glittering world to which I wanted to belong.

When I was eighteen, I moved to New York to attend the Parsons School of Design. I wasn't exactly green, I was chartreuse—but that's okay, because New York is all about either breaking or forming bright young things. At that time, Parsons' dorms were in the YMCA at Ninth Avenue and 34th Street. You cannot imagine a more humble beginning. I remember my parents walking down the hallway, and my mother exclaiming she felt like she was on a train compartment because the doors were so close together. Needless to say, she burst into tears when we walked into the room—a cell if there ever was one, but as they say, hunger makes you ambitious. The New York I dreamed of was actually Hollywood's 1930s interpretation: acres of marble floors, streamlined soigné interiors, and twinkly views. Alas, that was to elude me for several years.

My first apartment to myself was what we jokingly called "Rue Quatorze." At the time, Manhattan's 14th Street was deeply unfashionable—comprising mainly 99-cent stores, greasy spoons, and a particularly revolting seafood shop called "Oh Shrimp!" Its awful smell (still burned into my subconscious) forced me to cross the street to avoid it. Nevertheless, it was a glorious time. I had my first job, working for John Rosselli, and real life had begun. The apartment was crumbling and tiny, but I embraced it, affecting the look of a decaying English conservatory—with an emphasis on the word "decaying"—but there was a freedom in not caring, and I would not blink at having a cocktail party for fifty.

In 1998 my beloved sister Sarah and her new husband moved to New York, and we bought a wonderful town house together, which we still live in today. It was quite the sow's ear when we began renovations, but I was finally ready to unleash the *Top Hat* fantasies that had been swirling in my head since youth: zebra-upholstered doors, nickel and ebony parquet, pink satin walls, and my crowing glory—a 1930 glass bathroom/ballroom by David Adler found abandoned in a salvage warehouse in Chicago. It would turn out to be an arduous and at times painful process, but one that has provided years of pleasure and satisfaction. I suppose a lot like childbirth—and to that point, houses, in a way, are living things that need love and attention to flourish and shine. I like interiors that are animated and lively—and party-ready—because isn't that what life should be?

This is a book about dreams coming true; the curiosities in the rooms I have decorated; and the people, artists, and places that have inspired me. When all is said and done and I am long forgotten, maybe someone will find this book in a dusty library—if such a thing still exists—and glimpse a bit of the pleasure my life has given me. I want them to have the sensation of dancing across an MGM soundstage, silhouetted in a klieg light, because that was my intention with this book, a very personal blend of work and fantasy.

Miles Redd

66 The chinchilla clouds had drifted past now and outside the ... night was bright as day. 99
—F. Scott Fitzgerald, "The Diamond as Big as The Ritz"

66 Something from Joseph Conrad sprang to my mind, although I cannot seem to remember what it was at the time. Perhaps I likened myself to Kurtz in *The Heart of Darkness* when, far from the trading company offices in Europe, he was faced with the ultimate horror. I do remember imagining myself in a pith helmet and white linen jodpurs, my face enigmatic behind a veil of mosquito netting. **99**

—John Kennedy Toole, *A Confederacy of Dunces*

I

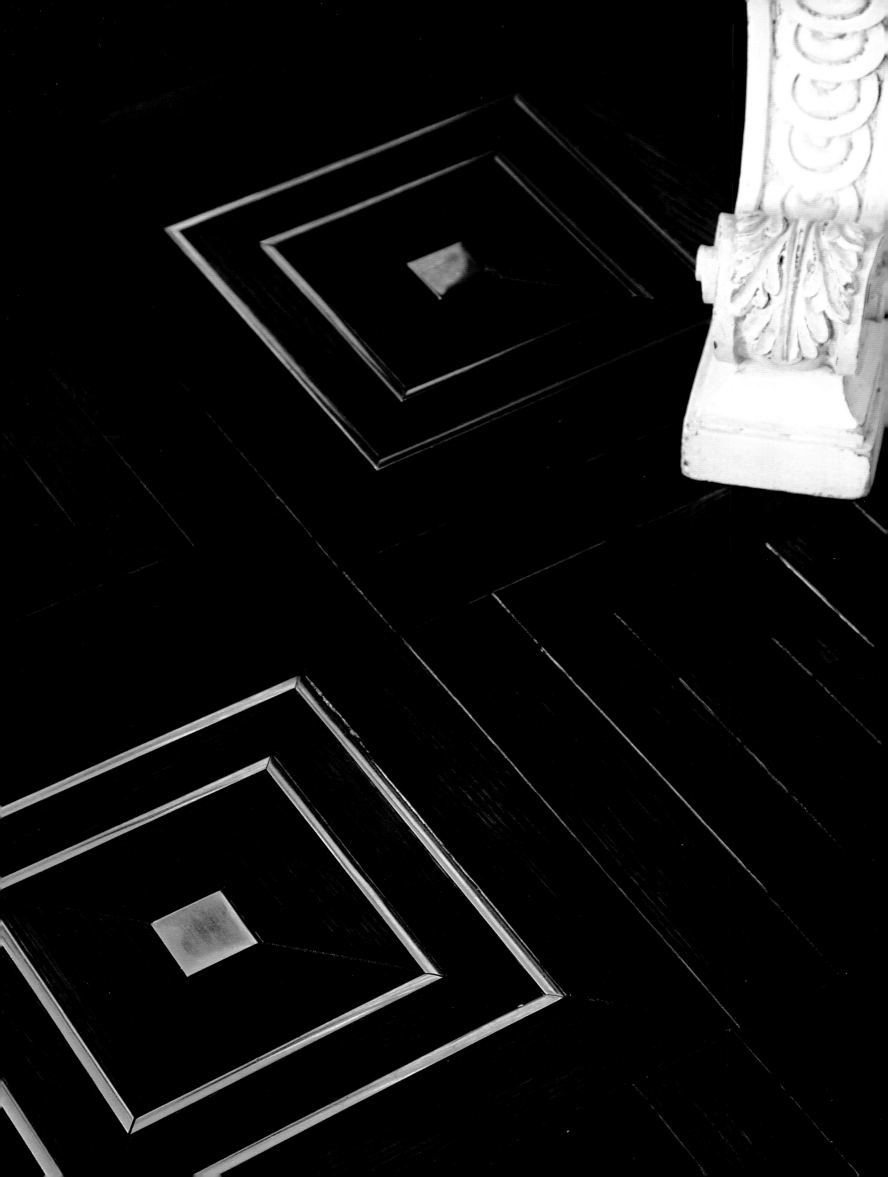

"To make a suitable setting for his collection, he then proceeded to pull down at Hampton the large plain house that Adam had built for his grandfather and to drag over to England stone by stone (as modern American millionaires are supposed to do) a Gothic French chateau. This he assembled round a splendid tower of his own designing, covered the walls of the rooms with French panelling and silks and set it in a formal landscape which he also designed and planted himself. It was all very grand and very mad, and in the between wars period of which I write, very much out of fashion."

—Nancy Mitford, *Love in a Cold Climate*

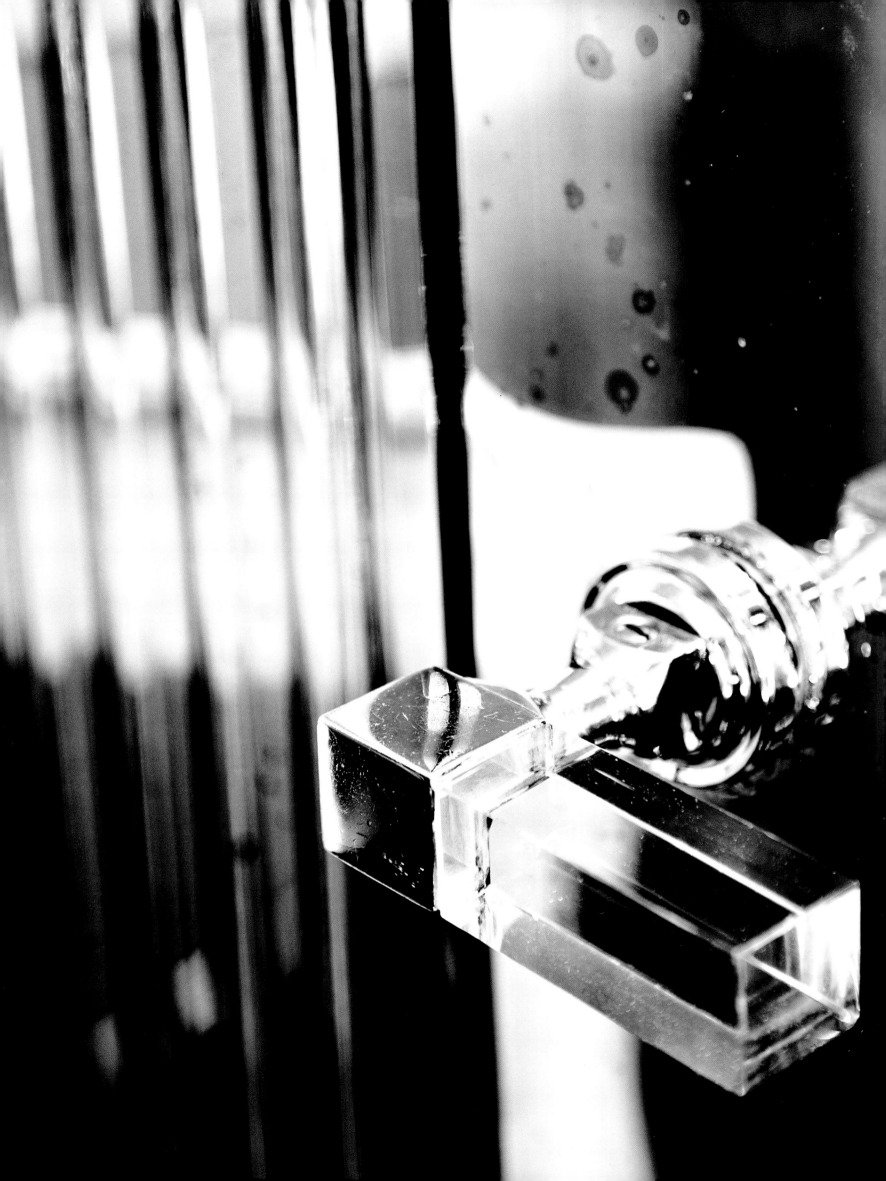

66 The pleasure of all bedrooms in good British colonial clubs—and Muthaiga is a fine example—is their enormous size and their spartan airiness. The doorways into these spaces are on an equally grand scale. There is also spare Indian-made custom furniture, circa 1930, an isolated washbasin along one wall, a water decanter, a hard floor of green or brown linoleum, and a luxurious bathroom, where the thundering of hot water echoes against the cream walls. 99

—James Fox, *White Mischief*

"They were racy, pleasure-loving, gala, good-looking Parisians who were part of the whole transition between the Edwardian era and the modern world. Money didn't seem to be of any importance to them, and they were wonderful in the way they surrounded us—not because of us, but because of the life they led— with fascinating people and events. All kinds of marvelous people came to the house..."

—Diana Vreeland, *D.V.*

"But I was in search of love in those days, and I went full of curiosity and the faint, unrecognized apprehension that here, at last, I should find that low door in the wall, which others, I knew, had found before me, which opened on an enclosed and enchanted garden, which was somewhere, not overlooked by any window, in the heart of that grey city."

—Evelyn Waugh, *Brideshead Revisited*

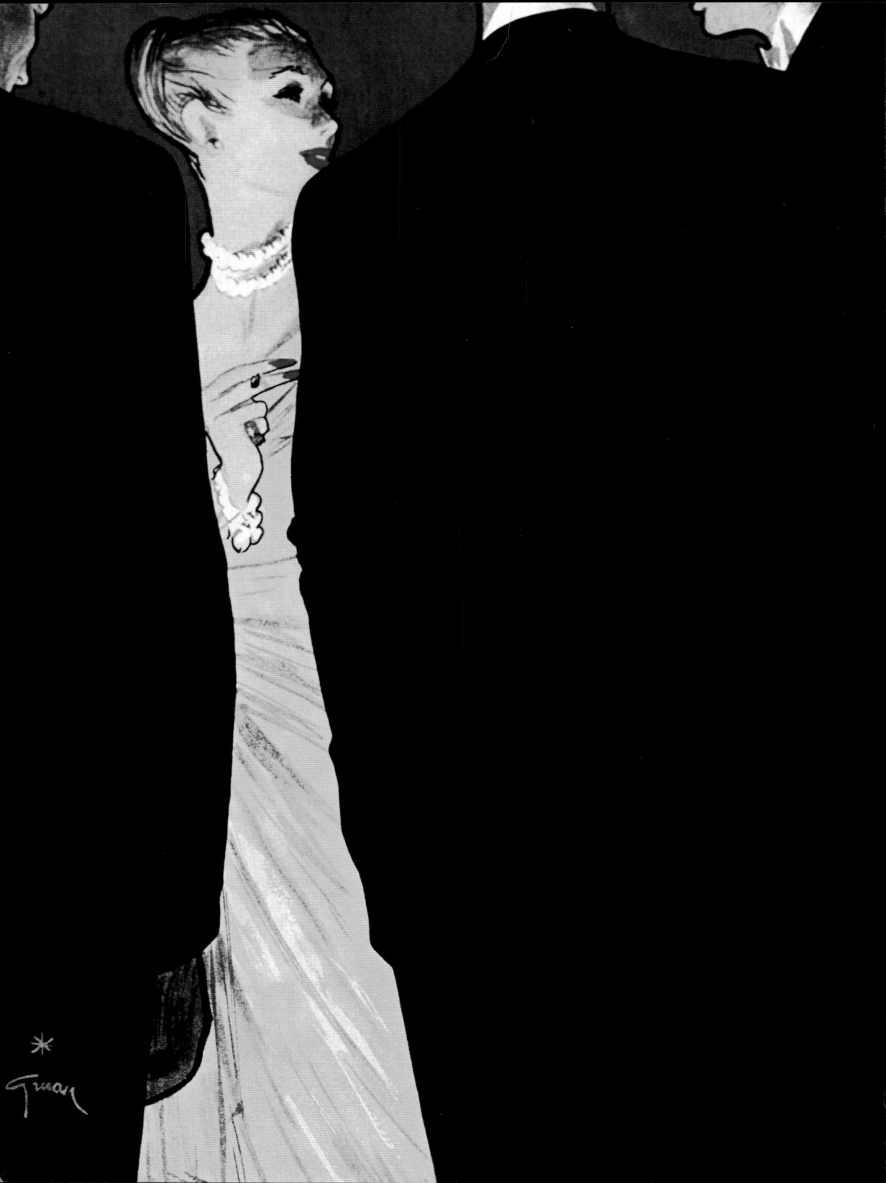

66 She was posing by the fireplace in the library on the second floor when she heard her husband's footsteps on the stairs. It was a graceful pose, inviting as the room itself, an unusual octagonal room with cinnamon lacquered walls, a yellow lacquered floor, brass bookshelves (a notion borrowed from Billy Baldwin), two huge bushes of brown orchids ensconced in yellow Chinese vases, a Marino Marini horse standing in a corner, a South Seas Gauguin over the mantel, and a delicate fire fluttering in the fireplace. French windows offered a view of a darkened garden, drifting snow and lighted tugboats floating like lanterns on the East River. A voluptuous couch, upholstered in mocha velvet, faced the fireplace, and in front of it, on a table lacquered the yellow of the floor, rested an ice-filled silver bucket; embedded in the bucket was a carafe brimming with pepper-flavored red Russian vodka. 99

—Truman Capote, "Mojave"

"I have no sense of possession. But to have no sense of possession is easier if you have owned a lot."

—Karl Lagerfeld

66 There is no excellent beauty that hath not some strangeness in the proportion. 99

—Francis Bacon

III

66 Here the air was warm and fragrant; the scent of flowers and fine linen mingled with the odor of cooked meats and truffles. Candle flames cast long gleams on rounded silver dish-covers; the clouded facets of the cut glass shone palely; there was a row of bouquets all down the table; and on the wide-bordered plates the napkins stood like bishops' mitres, each with an oval-shaped roll between its folds. Red lobster claws protruded from platters; oversized fruit was piled up on moss in openwork baskets; quail were served in their plumage; steam rose from open dishes... 99

IV

—Gustave Flaubert, *Madame Bovary*

DAVID ADLER

BYZANTIUM
Faith and Power (1261–1557)

BELLES LETTR

"It had snowed heavily in Paris the night before I went to the Bois de Boulogne to lunch with the Duke and Duchess of Windsor. Inside, burning logs and immense bouquets of forced spring blossoms dispelled all thoughts of chill. As in every home she has lived in, the duchess has made this Louis XVI mansion a highly personal creation. Large but crowded with collections, it manages to be chic and cozy, a word usually hard to come by in an atmosphere of such overwhelming elegance."

—Fleur Cowles, *Harper's Bazaar,* May 1966

V

"Mummy and Rory both had the same quality of innocence. The dark spots of life were discarded and not allowed to intrude on their existence. They saw the world through a golden haze and if you were lucky enough to be part of their magic circle they took you through into that fairyland where life was always fun and always filled with beauty. The reverse simply wasn't tolerated, or perhaps noticed."

— Pat Cavendish O'Neill, *A Lion in the Bedroom*

"Against the pale gold leather wall a quantity of white camellias were banked up in old mahogany flower stands, between them and at even distances, stood suits of armour, which shone with a cold glitter in the dimly lighted room."

—Ronald Firbank, "True Love"

VI

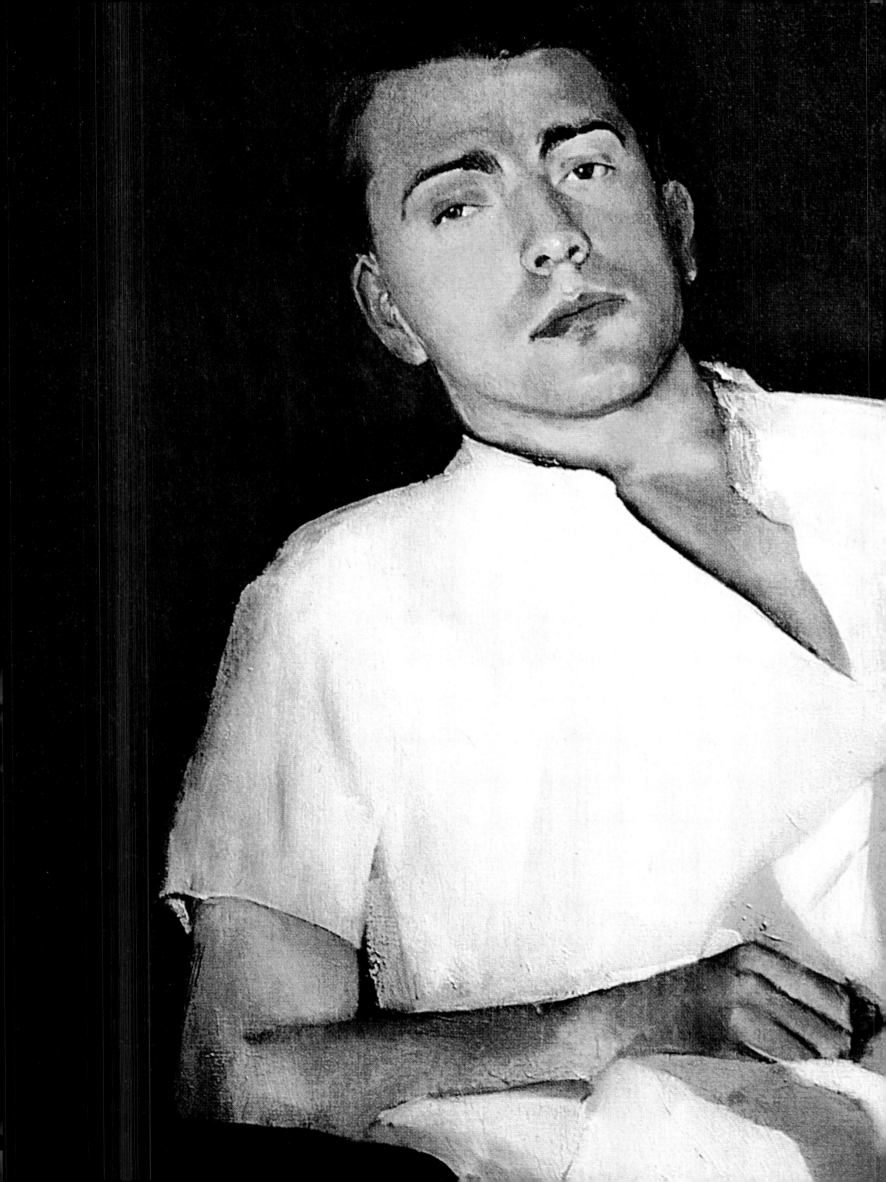

"Genius creates, and taste preserves. Taste is the good sense of genius; without taste, genius is only sublime folly."

—Alexander Pope

VII

PEACE AND WAR MEMORIAL

66 'Plender, get a bed made up for me downstairs.'
Plender and Wilcox exchanged an anxious glance.
'Very good, my lord. Which room shall we put it in?'
Lord Marchmain thought for a moment.
'The Chinese drawing-room; and, Wilcox, the "Queen's Bed".' 99

—Evelyn Waugh, *Brideshead Revisited*

"He was just a face I saw in a discotheque one winter, but it was I who ended up going back to Fire Island to pick up his things."

—Andrew Holleran, *Dancer From the Dance*

VIII

Jean Cocteau ✪

66 'Rosamond, dear! What are you doing here?'

'You invited me for the weekend, Stephen, don't you remember?'

'But how could you be so cruelly literal, darling?' 99

—Philip Hoare, *Serious Pleasures: The Life of Stephen Tennant*

"I know when to go out. And when to stay in. Get things done."

—David Bowie, "Modern Love"

IX

Vesuv

> **"There are chemists who spend their whole lives trying to find out what's in a lump of sugar. I want to know one thing. What is color?"**
>
> —Pablo Picasso

PICASSO: WOMEN

66 **For masterpieces are not single and solitary births; they are the outcome of many years of thinking in common, of thinking by the body of the people, so that the experience of the mass is behind the single voice.** 99

—Virginia Woolf, *A Room of One's Own*

COLEFAX & FOWLER

FARM LARKIN

THE GARDEN DESIGN SOURCEBOOK   David Stevens

VICTORIAN AMERICA   GARRETT · LARKIN

Harvey H. Kaiser   LANDMARKS
LANDSCAPE

> **"Experience is never limited, and it is never complete; it is an immense sensibility, a kind of huge spider-web, of the finest silken threads, suspended in the chamber of consciousness and catching every air-borne particle in its tissue."**
>
> —Henry James, "The Art of Fiction"

"We all owe a great debt to Cecil, for keeping the idea of style alive."

—David Bailey, quoted in *Cecil Beaton: Photographs 1920–1970*

XIII

(eci)
BeAToN's
New
York.

"Reginald closed his eyes with the elaborate weariness of one who has rather nice eyelashes and thinks it useless to conceal the fact."

—Saki, *Reginald*

> **Merlinford nestled in a valley of south-westerly aspect, among orchards and old mellow farmhouses.... It was a house to live in, not to rush out from all day to kill enemies and animals. It was suitable for a bachelor, or a married couple with one, or at most two, beautiful, clever, delicate children. It had Angelica Kauffman ceilings, a Chippendale staircase, furniture by Sheraton and Hepplewhite; in the hall there hung two Watteaus; there was no entrenching tool to be seen, nor the head of any animal.**
>
> —Nancy Mitford, *The Pursuit of Love*

“I prefer a good 'interior' to a good landscape. The impression has a greater intensity—the thing itself a more complex animation. I like fine old rooms that have been occupied in a fine old way.”

—Henry James, *Italian Hours*

"I had not been in Texas long before I started having millions of insights about the difference between Texas and the rest of America. I was going to write these insights down, but then I thought—Nahhh."

—Ian Frazier, *Nobody Better, Better Than Nobody*

"The opposite of luxury is not poverty because in the houses of the poor you can smell a good *pot au feu*. The opposite is not simplicity for there is beauty in the corn-stall and barn, often great simplicity in luxury, but there is nothing in vulgarity, its complete opposite."

—Coco Chanel, as quoted by Cecil Beaton, in *Beaton in the Sixties: The Cecil Beaton Diaries as He Wrote Them, 1965-1969*

"Erect, isolated, flanked by her husband and myself, the Duchess kept to the left of the staircase, already wrapped in her Tiepolo cloak, her throat clasped in its band of rubies, devoured by the eyes of women and men alike, who sought to divine the secret of her beauty and distinction."

—Marcel Proust, *Remembrance of Things Past*

66 **Perhaps the charm, attraction, character, call it what you will, of the house is that it has grown over the years in a haphazard sort of way.** 99

—The Duchess of Devonshire, *Chatsworth: The House*

66 I was taken to my room. It was a largish attic-room with beams appearing in unexpected places and a ceiling that followed the contours of the roof.... Not a conventional bedroom judged by English standards.... However, it delighted me because its walls were hung with the most brilliant scarlet linen.... It must, I think, have been the same material as that described by Proust in the sitting-room of Tansonville 'of so vivid a scarlet that it would catch fire if a single sun-ray touched it.' 99

—Lord Berners, *The Château de Résenlieu*

XVII

66 'I wonder you don't take Elliott's furniture over with you.'

'I don't think it would be very suitable. I shall make it all modern, with perhaps just a little touch of Mexican here and there to give it a note. As soon as I get to New York I'll find out who is the decorator everyone's going to now.' **99**

—W. Somerset Maugham, *The Razor's Edge*

66 Now that she was alone in it she began to be aware of the extreme beauty of the room, a grave and solemn beauty which penetrated her. It was very high, rectangular in shape, with grey boiseries and cherry-coloured brocade curtains.... This was a civilized interior, it had nothing to do with out of doors. Every object in it was perfect. The furniture had the severe lines and excellent proportions of 1780, there was a portrait by Lancret of a lady with a parrot on her wrist, a bust of the same lady by Bouchardon, a carpet like the one in Linda's flat, but larger and grander, with a huge coat of arms in the middle. A high carved bookcase contained nothing but French classics bound in contemporary morocco, with the Sauveterre crest, and, open on a map table, lay a copy of Redouté's roses. 99

—Nancy Mitford, *The Pursuit of Love*

"But Charlie, don't forget what happened to the man who suddenly got everything he always wanted.... He lived happily ever after."

—Willy Wonka, *Willy Wonka and the Chocolate Factory,* 1971

Thank you to all the people who helped make this book possible: Kim Alker, Prosper and Martine Assouline, Randall Bachner, Quentin Bacon, John Beitel, Fernando Bengoechea, Matt Bernardo, Erin Black, Alex and Eliza Bolen, Dick Bories, Hamish Bowles, Blake Brunson, Temo Callahan, Dara Caponigro, Lauren Carras, Howard Christian, Paul and Sara Costello, Oscar and Annette de la Renta, Stephen Drucker, Camille Dubois, Kara Dusenbury, Brian and Tracey Early, Ethan and Dania Early, Doug Friedman, Furlow Gatewood, Amanda Gentilcore, Oberto Gili, Wendy Goodman, Larry and Lorna Graev, Crystal Granberry, David Haag, François Halard, Austin Harrelson, Kevin Harter and Jangir Sultan, Leslie Hearn, Juan Herrera, Rand and Lindsay Holstead, Agustin Hurtado, David Kaihoi, David Kaiser, Jihyun Kim, Esther Kremer, Cameron Krone, Ana and Philippe Laffont, Francesco Lagnese, Amber Laign, Eduardo Larrea, Robert A. Lisak, Thomas Loof, Amalia Lora, Mariann Maher, Ronnie Martin, Sarah and Bobby McCain, Miles McCain, Jack McCain, George McCain, Marian McEvoy, Tom Mendenhall and James Scully, James Merrill, Mike Milillo, Keith Moorman, Jennifer and Dominic Moross, Senga Mortimer, Nasser Nakib, Deborah Needleman, David and Liz Netto, Wright and Valerie Ohrstrom, Nick Olsen, Euclides Pagan, Chris Pearson, Chassie Post, Norris Post, Sue and Buddy Redd, Danielle Rollins, Glen Rollins, John Rosselli, Bret Rudy, Margaret Russell, Allison Sarofim, Fayez Sarofim, Anita Sarsidi, Gil Schafer, Sloan Scherr and Patrick Moore, Alex Schlempp, Fritz von der Schulenburg, Ken Selody, James Shearron, Mimi Crume Sterling, Rene and Barbara Stoeltie, Martyn Thompson, Newel Turner, Tom and Mila Tuttle, Simon Upton, Miguel Flores Vianna, John Weinstein, Liz and Steve Weinstein, Susan Wilcox, Bunny Williams, Anna Wintour, Martha Young, Guillermo Zalamea, and to all of my clients, past and present. Thanks also to *Architectural Digest, Country Life, Domino, Elle Decor, House & Garden, House Beautiful, New York Magazine, Town & Country, Veranda, Vogue,* and *W.*

PHOTO CREDITS